Welcome to the home of

::::::::::::::::::::::::::::::::::::::::::::::::::::::::::::::::::::::::::::::::::::::::::

# Welcome

Friends and family...treasured guests...special times and special people. Our moments together pass so quickly, but the memories last forever. Capture and save those memories in the pages of this guest book. Invite and encourage your guests to write down their thoughts, feelings, reminiscences, or wishes on this day. Let them be inspired by the heart-warming quotations throughout the book and invite them to write as much or as little as they'd like. In the years to come, you'll be flooded with wonderful memories each time you open and read this guest book. It will remain a cherished family reminder of very meaningful times.

The voice of the sea
     speaks to the soul.

KATE CHOPIN

I warmed both hands
before the fire of life.

WALTER SAVAGE LANDOR

Sounds of the wind or sounds of the sea
Make me happy just to be.

JUNE POLIS

How beautiful it is                    to be alive!

HENRY SEPTIMUS SUTTON

The best kind of friend is the kind you
can sit on a porch swing with,
never say a word, then walk away
feeling like it was the best conversation
you ever had.

UNKNOWN

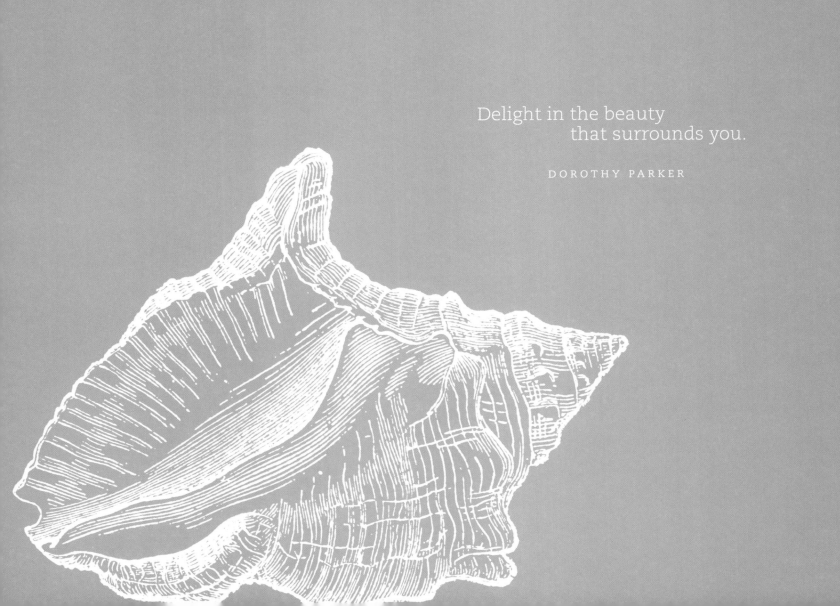

Delight in the beauty
that surrounds you.

DOROTHY PARKER

Gratitude is a twofold love—
love coming to visit us,
and love running out
to greet a welcome guest.

HENRY VAN DYKE

All day, where the sunlight
played on the seashore,
Life sat.

OLIVE SCHREINER

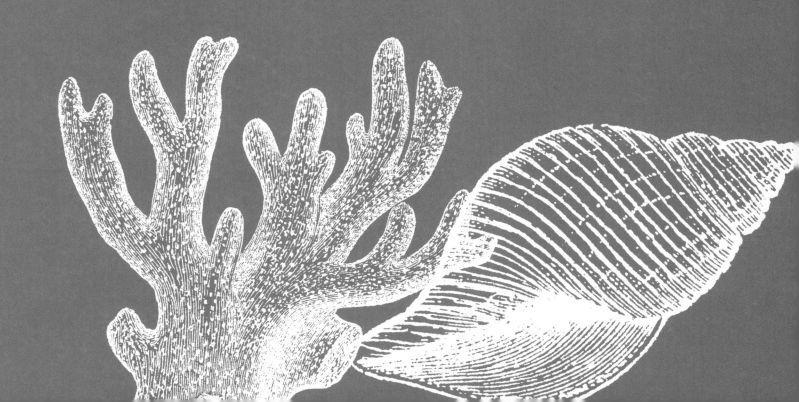

The most precious things of life
are near at hand...

JOHN BORROUGHS

Live in the sunshine,
swim the sea,
drink the wild air...

RALPH WALDO EMERSON

Nothing valuable can be lost
by taking time.

ABRAHAM LINCOLN

When I count my blessings,
I count you twice.

IRISH PROVERB

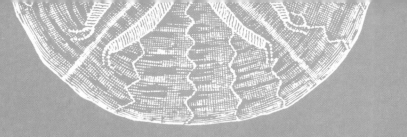

The time to relax is when
  you don't have time for it.

SYDNEY J. HARRIS

The joy that you give to others
is the joy that comes back to you.

JOHN GREENLEAF WHITTIER

Now and then
   it's good to pause
in our pursuit of happiness
         and just be happy.

GUILLAUME APOLLINAIRE

The day, water, sun, moon, night—
I do not have to purchase
these things with money.

PLAUTUS

The day is emptying its pockets,
laying out, one by one,
all its possessions.

JÁNOS PILINSZKY

Every time we walk along a beach
    some ancient urge disturbs us
            so that we find ourselves
    shedding shoes and garments
or scavenging among seaweed
        and whitened timbers...

LOREN EISELEY

Any time not spent on beachcombing,
fishing, friendship or love
is squandered.

UNKNOWN

Nothing ever tasted any better
than a cold beer on a beautiful
afternoon with nothing to look forward
to but more of the same.

HUGH HOOD

Have a good time, relax, and enjoy.
Feel that you want to repeat it.
Desire to share it with those who
are important to you.

STAN GASSMAN

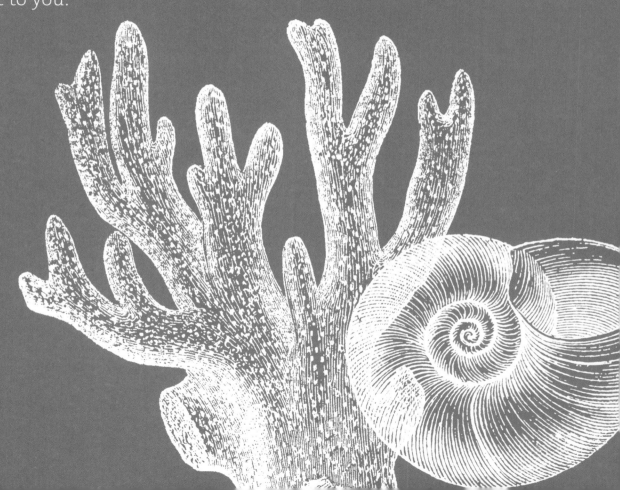

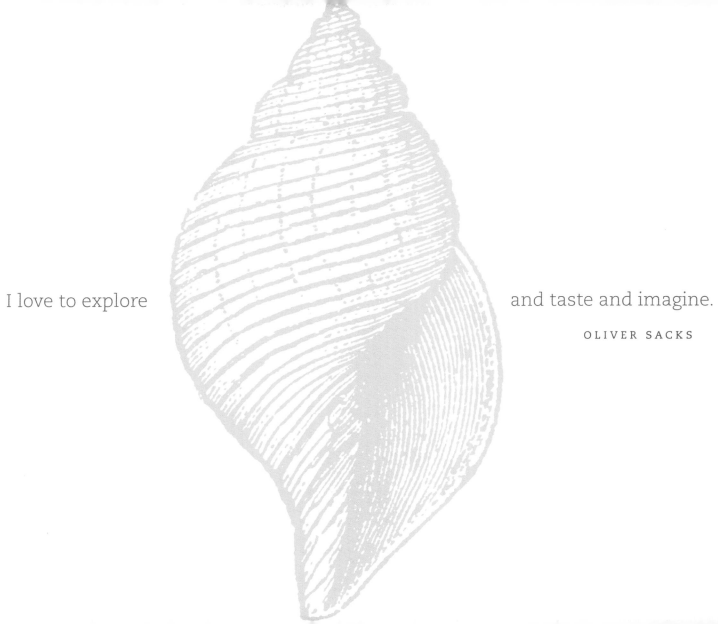

I love to explore and taste and imagine.

OLIVER SACKS

If you were a bird, and lived on high,
    You'd lean on the wind when the wind came by,
You'd say to the wind when it took you away:
    "That's where I wanted to go today!"

A.A. MILNE

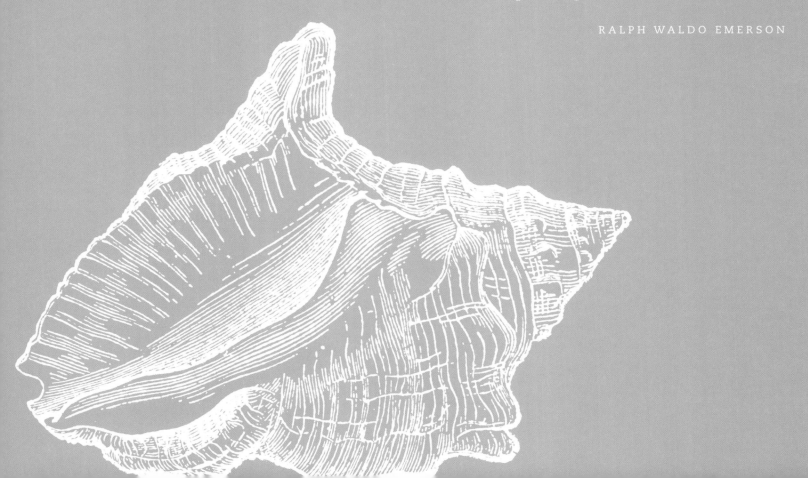

Adopt the pace of nature…

RALPH WALDO EMERSON

Nibblin' on sponge cake
    Watching the sun bake
All of those tourists covered with oil
    Strummin my six-string
       On my front porch swing
Smell those shrimp they're beginnin' to boil.

JIMMY BUFFETT

No day is so bad
it can't be fixed with a nap.

CARRIE SNOW

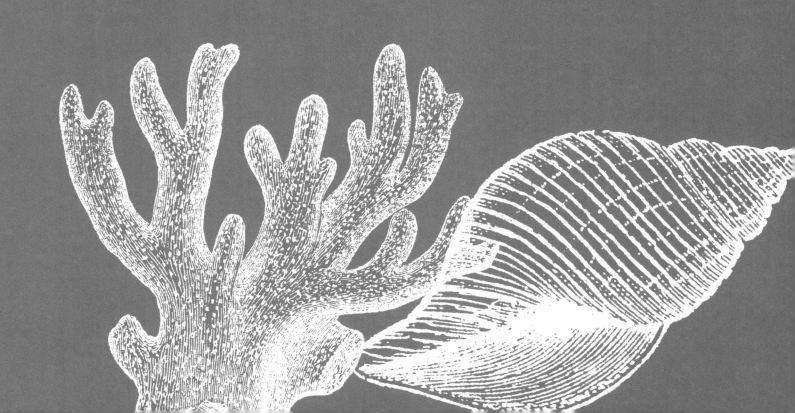

What is life if, full of care,
    we have no time to stand and stare?

W.H. DAVIES

...go to the window
and look at the stars.

RALPH WALDO EMERSON

There is absolutely no reason
   for being rushed along with the rush.
Everybody should be free to go slow.

ROBERT FROST

Sit outside at midnight and close your eyes;
feel the grass, the air, the space.
Listen to birds for ten minutes at dawn.
Memorize a flower.

LINDA HASSELSTROM

Sit in reverie and watch the
changing color of the waves
that break upon the idle seashore
of the mind.

HENRY WADSWORTH LONGFELLOW

Stress cannot exist
   in the presence of a pie.

DAVID MAMET

Time has fallen asleep
   in the afternoon sunshine.

ALEXANDER SMITH

Let tomorrow come tomorrow.

ALICE STEINBACH

Don't worry, be happy.

BOBBY MCFERRIN

Special times, special places,
special friends together.
The moments pass so quickly.
But the memories last forever.

UNKNOWN